Handbook for Marketing Students

Best tips and strategies

Nigel Aksel

First Edition

Published in Amazon.com

Nigel Aksel
Handbook for Marketing Students: Best Student Tips
and Terms, 2019

1st Edition
All Rights Reserved
ISBN: 9781090514530

Table of Content

Tables

Dedication

I want to dedicate this book to my marketing students Abylaykhan, Adilet, Aknur, Asem, Balnur, Irina, Karina, Konstantin, Murat, Nurbolat, Nursultan, Rakhat, Symbat and Ulzhan. I am glad that they made a choice in marketing as their specialization and want to become the best specialists of the region. I am thanking them for their class participation and wish them the best marketing journey in their professional life.

This book is for them and many other students to become the best professional of their countries in marketing.

For whom is this book written?

I noticed that many books in my shelf are for applicants or for job seekers. The idea came to write a book for marketing students and help them succeed in their university and professional life.

Generally, this book will be useful for marketing students, applicants, interns, specialists and professionals. I also included tips for professors who can utilize this book in their teaching and motivating students in their specializations. And, in addition, parents can also learn how to understand their children and support them in studies and various situations.

Moreover, this book also for entrepreneurs, businessmen, government specialists who are focusing on marketing activities, communication, research and want to hire the best specialists for the development of their economies and organizations.

All of them will love reading this handbook for many tips and strategies.

Introduction

Most of my students I noticed want to achieve their success in life very fast and to live a better life as soon as possible. They are busy with many activities and businesses. Those who achieved a preliminary success are the happiest. Unfortunately, I saw many students, who believe that education and research in marketing are not so important. But I do not know whether they are right or wrong now. And I also cannot push them if they have their own priorities in personal life, businesses or families.

My purpose, as a lecturer, to help and direct them in marketing specialization. For me it is important to provide them with the most significant tips and techniques that will help them to understand marketing during and after their classes, graduation and in professional life. It will help them to achieve a greater triumph in the field of marketing, a specialization they selected at the beginning of their professional journey.

Indeed, marketing is not a game for anybody, it is a real chance to achieve some goals or not, especially for your organization or economy. With marketing tips and strategies, you must acquire the rules and methods of the market economy and how to use them to take the maximum opportunity to become the greatest marketing professional for your company or own business.

This book can teach you how to craft the rules of marketing by heart and love them, using every day.

I strongly believe that you will be our top marketing students, who will benefit in future for our businesses and economic development of our region.

Structure of the Book

The book consists of sections and they are grouped in the way that you can directly open your own section, depending on your marketing status or relation to the student. To illustrate, this book has the following sections for the marketing student:

1) Marketing student
2) Marketing intern
3) Marketing applicant
4) Marketing specialist
5) Marketing professional

The first section includes tips for a marketing student. The second one - for an intern when you have to work and practice. The third one – for a graduate, who wants to search for a job. The forth one – for a specialist, who is working as a manager in the company and wants to become the best professional. The last one for a professional, who has more than 5 years of experience in marketing to become a guru in marketing.

The book also adds some value in many student activities too. The following list shows the structure for other sections:

1. Marketing Terms
2. Marketing Strategies
3. Marketing Plan
4. Marketing Tests
5. How to questions?
6. Marketing Test

In first section, you can find general terms of marketing, which will help any reader to understand the scope of marketing. In the second section, you can find marketing strategies for your company to succeed. In the third section, you can find tips and terms for planning. In other units, which starts on "how", you can find necessary instructions on how to show the exceptional performance in writing, reading, presentations etc. At the end, you will find a sample test to check your marketing knowledge after the reading of this book.

Parents, professors and professionals can also use this book as a handbook to direct their children, students or specialists in different situations. There are some ideas for them to support their students in many ways.

Marketing Student

As a marketing student, you can benefit from many contents of this book at various stages of your marketing career.

As the first step, you can find tips and terms necessary when you are a student. Let's start and check them out.

1. Define Your Goals

Analyze, think and define your goals. Your long-term goals, not for one week or a month.

Usually, I ask my students to write 5-10-year goals and present them in the class. It is very important, especially, if they are planning to become a marketing professional in the future. The earlier they define their goals, the earlier they will start preparing for realization of their goal.

Generally, all students have some ideas for the future. But it is important for them to set their goals, which are specific and professional. So, they will be motivated for planning their future from the first day at the university.

In realization of any goal, marketing skills are very important. For example, to analyze the trends, markets, yourself, your character and your journey from the right point.

It is also important to set up clear goals and focus on the most important, which means to do priorities of your goals.

In my classes I try to help my students to define their primary goals. For me, it is important to understand my students' priorities and help them to achieve their goals by involving them in activities of the class work, lectures and seminars.

As a practical part, let me show a sample table for defining student's goals.

Table 1 Goals Plan of the Marketing Student

	Goals	Deadline
Goal 1		
Goal 2		
Goal 3		

Goal 4		
Goal 5		
Goal 6		
Goal 7		
Goal 8		
Goal 9		
Goal 10		

The table 1 is simple and takes almost no time. In the second column, you should write your goals and in the next one - the deadlines for your goals.

It is actually, not about the writing goal but to see when you have to achieve them in order to plan.

For homework, let me ask you to do the following task.

Task: Build your goal table as in the sample table above.

2. Plan your future

Analyze over your goals and plan how to achieve them. Planning is important for realization of your goals with the best outcome for you.

Planning will help you to reach your goals step by step. It means that you will set and divide your goals into tasks and actions for a period between now and your defined future.

I recommend students to do a real plan of the future. In the table 2 you can see a sample plan.

Table 2 Sample Future Plan of the Marketing Student

#	Sections of Plan	Deadline	Activities
1	Education		
1.1	Bachelor		
	Courses		
	Internship		
	Diploma Thesis		
1.2	Master		

	Courses		
	Internship		
	Diploma Thesis		
1.3	PhD		
2	Language		
2.1	English		
2.2	Other		
3	Software		
4	Hardware		
5	Speaking		
6	Writing		
7	Volunteer		
8	Research		
9	Job Application		
10	Other		

This plan will help you to see the scope of your work and prepare for achieving your goals, doing it step by step, deadline by deadline.

Without planning you will not see the future and you will focus only on present issues and activities. It will limit you in focus and professional career.

For now, please accomplish task 2 as a homework. This will help you to plan your future from now.

Task 2: Build your future plan as in the sample table above.

3. Buy a notebook

Marketing students work a lot and do research, searching for information. Most of the information are available on internet.

Without your own computer you will waste time visiting libraries and internet cafes.

With your own notebook, you can save time and do your research from any place. You can also do your surveys and send your questionnaires to the staff of the companies easily.

I bought my notebook for my own money. Try to earn your money first and buy yourself. There are some hints also to earn your money in this book. You can also check my other books for investment and tips for promotion.

4. Improve Business Communication Skills

Every day, marketing specialists communicate with customers, partners, suppliers, government people and many others.

Therefore, as a student you have to learn effectively to communicate with various people to achieve the purpose. You have to learn many communication tools and channels to achieve your goals.

For example, you have to learn how to work on complains, advertising messages and with international cultures. It is important to communicate in various tones, languages and with different levels of management.

5. Improve Speaking Skills

Marketing students should practice speaking in classes. They are future managers and have to talk to people and experts in forums, conferences and make presentations for their potential customers, partners, experts and employees.

Therefore, as a student you have to practice speaking as much as possible. You can do it first in front of a mirror or in front of your family. There are some tips for preparation of the presentation in this book below too.

6. Improve Writing Skills

Without writing skills, it is difficult to write convincing messages, letters and reports.

Students should practice writing at classes and home. You have to write your ideas clearly and precisely. You can find an additional section on how to improve writing in this book also.

7. Improve Research Skills

Marketing Specialists should constantly research for new information and prepare reports. They have to learn how to research companies, markets and industries, including stock and commodity markets.

Check out some tips to increase your researcher ranking in this book below.

8. Learn new global languages

Marketing students have to learn new languages as they have to work in many new markets abroad.

First, they have to constantly research international markets; second, they have to communicate with people from international markets; and third, they have to do business.

As a priority, students should learn English language and other main languages.

9. Explore cultures of various nations and countries

Marketing specialists have to work with specialists and customers from different countries. Each country has its own values, traditions and cultural peculiarities. For students, it is important to learn new cultural differences to avoid marketing losses while implementing country scale and global marketing campaigns.

10. Advance your software skills

Marketers work with a lot of data for analysis, grouping, selecting etc. Each marketing managers have to learn new software skills for analysis, statistics and for preparing marketing reports.

Many of them are creative and work with graphical or video editing software, so that they can create infographics and video spots for TV.

As a student, it is important to learn new software products and practice them in different real projects.

11. Involve in projects

Any university is a good place to prepare a business plan or project, including with the professor.

Interested students can join volunteer projects, scholarship competitions, contests and other projects.

Students can also join grant projects with their professors. Below you can check out some tips for project participation and funding.

12. Read professional books

Marketing specialists should use their time to read professional books on different subjects and areas of business.

This will help them expand their knowledges and increase efficiency of marketing strategies and plans.

Please check also some tips for reading below.

13. Exchange or Study Abroad Programs

Today, perspective students have a choice to participate in multiple exchange programs. This is an opportunity to improve language and cultural skills, learn new markets and educational approaches.

In addition, you can receive a second certificate or diploma from university abroad, which will be a good element of the resume for your job application.

14. Learn and define your internship company

Many students start to prepare for their internships very late. And they are not able to do internship in the best companies of the region. So, it is important for them to research companies for the future internship as earlier as possible.

They can start communicating with companies on many terms, including for doing research, preparation of new marketing plan or marketing campaign.

If a company will be interested in research and marketing plan, a student has a good chance to get an internship and after it even a job.

15. Learn and plan your job application as early as possible

For a last year student, it is also important to start a job application process as early as possible.

Finding a job will require another internship or several application processes. On the other hand, you have to learn your own potential and evaluation on getting the right job with the appropriate salary and social packages.

16. Participate actively in organizational work

Many universities offer a number of activities for participation in various events, seminars, contests, speaking clubs, where students can improve their organizational, communication and networking skills.

Try your best to be in the center of these events and promotion campaigns of your university. You will learn a valuable experience for your future career.

17. Do sport activities

During university, students read a lot, sit in the chair long hours, worry about exams and many other.

For that, they have a good medicine – sport clubs. They must involve in various sport activities such as football, volleyball, swimming, running, martial arts etc.

As option, students can do morning and evening exercises every day at home or at university sport clubs.

It will help them stay fit and in positive mood.

18. Make a lot of friends

Studying is a hard time for many students, especially when you have a lot of subjects. And sometimes stressful, especially during exam weeks or study abroad programs. For students, it is healthy to be in good mood and in positive attitude. This will help to succeed.

Therefore, you should make a lot of friends to share your kitchen, books, assist each other in various situations. It will help you to save time and learn how to support each other in homework, studies, student life etc.

19. Allocate time for theaters, museum etc.

To understand people, business and social environments, students should also spend time in public places such as museums, theaters, exhibitions and many other places to learn history, arts, cultural activities etc.

It will help them to see emotions, learn people and their tastes, also to test various services and their quality.

For marketing specialist, this will expand horizons in understanding markets and social needs.

20. Do day planning well

Day planning differs from long term and strategic planning of the student. It helps you to prioritize your workday.

Day plan is organization of the day in order to be punctual, do time management and succeed.

Below, you can see a sample day plan I recommend my students.

Table 3 Sample Day Plan

Time	Activity	Place
07:00	Wake up	
07:05	Washing	
07:10	Morning Exercises	
07:30	Prepare Breakfast	
07:45	Breakfast	
08:15	Check you emails/plan for a day	
08:30	Way to University	
09:00	Start your day at university	
13:00	Lunch Time	
14:00	Continue at University	
16:00	Library	
18:00	Dinner	
19:00	Sport Activities	

21:00	Homework preparation	
23:00	Go to bed	

It is important for a student to follow the day plan to meet all the deadlines in time.

If you have an online or mobile calendar it is even better. You can fix your meetings and classes easily and plan your day effectively online.

Marketing Intern

Internship is one of the key periods of the student's path to the future. It is a time to contribute and show in practice how to do marketing for a target company.

In many situations, your company will be interested to purchase an idea or program of the student and offer a job after the internship.

Here, you can find tips and terms necessary for marketing students to succeed during the internship period. Let's check them out.

1. On your first meeting, discuss with a company supervisor the challenging issues and trends and how you can help the company to achieve its goals in marketing.
2. Be punctual and in-time, and start your internship day like many other colleagues.
3. Be curious, ask questions on various issues and topics of the company. In many cases employees can tell you

many interesting facts and plans of the company.

4. Make a clear plan of internship with deadlines. They have to be realistic to achieve your results.

5. Learn your internship company well. Start with organizational structure, documentation such as business plan, statue, contracts etc. Learn its products and services, their pricing, costs and features. Then processes, production, equipment, target markets.

6. Visit markets, including supermarkets or special business areas to check how the products or services of the company purchased or sold. Understand the points of sales.

7. Learn competitive products and services, their pricing, features, terms of delivery, terms of payment, pre and after sales services etc.

8. Analyze the partners and their role in creating the value chain.

9. Collect data and classify. Compare data with the data of the competitors.
10. You can organize surveys of clients, partners and employees to receive some ideas and facts for the development of the company. This should be a strong ground of your marketing report and project.
11. Write in detail your internship report.
12. If your internship company does not have a marketing plan, it is better to offer your company to prepare a marketing plan.
13. Prepare your company internship report including the marketing plan.
14. Depending on your schedule, your marketing plan can be focused on particular product or market.
15. Include your analysis, marketing strategies, recommendations and marketing campaign plan for 1 year. You can do it for 3 years as well.
16. If your internship company is interested in development of its

international presence or enter new markets, you can offer to develop an international business plan, for example, for 3 years.

17. For the best export products, you can analyze potential 3 countries as the first step and build an entry strategy for the company. You have to analyze various strategies of international marketing and use your communication skills to get the right information from the target country. The best solution will be if you can find a reliable local partner who will be interested in creating a joint venture with your internship company. It will decrease risks and lower the cost of entry for your company.

18. Make sure that you have prepared power point presentation to present in front of the management, supervisor, your university supervisor

and other students and staff of the internship company.

19. Prepare for your internship presentation. In many cases, internship presentation will be counted as a final thesis presentation of the student. There are some tips for preparation of your presentation in the book below.

20. Make sure that you have practiced several times to present your materials in front of your colleagues, family members or classmates.

21. Prepare a list of questions, which might be asked by the Audience, Attestation or Diploma Committee. Prepare answers for these questions and imagine how you will answer to questions. Practice in front of the mirror and after ask somebody to be in a role of the committee.

22. Present your report, marketing plan and thesis with the highest confidence and be ready to answer

questions and show additional materials.

23. Prepare to ask several questions from the company people and management. For example, how they like your strategy or presentation offer.

24. Make sure that your presentation shows several options for selection by the internship company. For example, several strategies for entry a new market can include: 1) join venture; 2) representative; 3) distributor. Each option can be with its own budget, costs, etc. So, the company will select the one option.

25. You have to organize a flow of your presentation in the way that at the end of your presentation, the internship company will be interested to invite you to realize offered strategy or plan for you and your team. So, you will get your job as one option!

26. Do not forget thanking all the members and show your readiness to the company to finish a project with the highest outcome.

Marketing Applicant

After your studies and graduation ceremony, you will receive your diploma.

Now, you are a marketing specialist. Congratulation!

But you have to do a lot of work and start your path to grow as a professional specialist in future.

In the case you showed the best result in your internship company, you will have a good chance to get your dream job there.

If it is not the case, you should not worry about it. You have to understand that you had an excellent opportunity and experience in your internship company and in university. Now, you will have many chances to find your best place for work in your new company.

In any case you can ask your recommendation letter from your internship supervisor for your future job application processes.

The following strategies should help you to get prepared for your job application processes after completing your education.

1. Request from your supervisors recommendation letters and ask them to describe your best strengths as a marketing specialist.

2. Prepare your initiative cover letter, stating your intentions, interests, strengths for your new job. You can use it in future as a sample, if you are planning to apply many other companies. However, it requires adaptation of your sample letter and resume, to make it specific for each company situation and plans.

3. Prepare a list of interview questions and practice yourself.

4. Prepare a list of required priorities from the company for you to join and be ready to ask questions during the interview to clarify the conditions and terms of the company. Learn the website in order to decide to send your

resume to a particular company. Do not waste time if the company is not interesting for you.

5. Update your resume and make sure to include your details of marketing experience in the internship company.

6. Prepare a list of companies where you can send your adapted resumes and recommendation letters.

7. You can also attend various international and local job fairs, join university alumni club or register in job exchange for open vacancies.

8. Research companies in detail, where you want to send your resume and cover letter. Eliminate your companies, which are not interesting for you at the moment.

9. Update your cover letter adapting it to the target company. It is important that you will address the company issues and offer your competences for

achieving or resolving the company situation.

10. Send your cover letter and resume via email to the organizations from your compiled list. You can also send your emails to the open vacancies of the companies, which you added from the job portals and web-sites.

11. In many cases you will get a call from a company. Expect to answer to all questions and ask 2-3 questions too.

12. Do not forget sending a thanking letter for a chance to be interviewed. This calling person later may be recommending your candidacy for the final decision by the management.

13. Start preparing for your interview by reviewing a company information.

14. Learn the title and full name of the person who will be interviewing you. Additionally, you can learn a biography of the experts to build the right dialogue during the interview. It is important to address the person by

name and also prepare specific questions that will be interesting for the interviewing specialist.

15. Be in time, if possible 15-20 minutes before the appointed interview time.

16. Make a breath excise to calm down and focus on the company and positiveness.

17. During the interview. Be confident, precise and short to show your competence. Make some notes and marks if necessary and point out your views and offers at the end of the interview.

18. Be realistic and tell what you know and can do for the company without exaggeration and deception.

19. After interview, do not forget to send a thank you letter again. You can add some remembering points, which you missed during the interview. Anyway, be positive and wait.

20. If you will get the job after your first interview, you are lucky. And try do

the best to realize your dream job in your company.

21. In many companies, on average, it can take 2-3 interviews to get a decision of the management. Be prepared for other interviews.

22. And in many cases, you have to visit 5-10 companies for interviews to be selected for your best place or career.

Remember, planning is the best tool to get the best job. Plan your job application accordingly.

Marketing Specialist

After your successful application process, you are now a marketing specialist of your company. It is a starting point to become a marketing professional. Congratulations!!!

As a marketing specialist of your company, start applying your knowledges and experiences from the first day of your work.

You are a valuable source of information as a marketing specialist to contribute for the development of your company.

Let me provide you also with tips and strategies to become a professional marketing specialist:

1) Begin from analyzing market prices. Let me give you an example. After my bachelor graduation, I joined one of Joint Venture companies, which had just launched a production line for selling noodles and fast food. The products were planned to enter the market after 1 month. My task was to

do marketing and provide the best sales strategy for the company. To do so, the first 3 months I spent 20-30% of my time, including weekends, in wholesale and retail markets. I analyzed prices, making notes in the excel sheet every week. You can check the example of my price analysis sheet below.

Table 4 Sample Price Analysis Sheet

Markets	Product	Prices per unit	Wholesale price

2) Start talking and surveying wholesalers and retails.

Let me provide you with an example. After joining my joint venture, I visited markets not just for price analysis, but also to talk to wholesalers and retailers, sometimes surveying them about the products, packages, pricing etc.

I used a notebook for surveying the wholesalers and retailers. The structure of it looked like the following:

Table 5 Sample Survey Table

	Wholesaler 1	Retailer 1
Full name		
Market		
Location of the booth		
Monthly sales		
Main suppliers		
Main products		
Conditions in the booth		
Payment Terms		

3) Introduce about your company.

Let me give you an example too. Before starting talking and asking anything I was introducing my company and products. Sellers were interested, when I was telling them that I am a marketing specialist of the production company and that they will receive pricing from the factory, which located in the region.

One day, when I was introducing my products to one of the wholesalers, he was so interested that he said: "Hey body, I will buy all products from the factory, if you will make me delivery". He also added that he would pay weekly for the sum delivered.

So, when I came to my company and explained my chairman, he was so happy that he increased my salary 4 times and provided me with a car and mobile telephone. He also asked me that I have to make a contract with him.

I did the contract and first supply very soon. This wholesaler continued to work even I left the company later.

4) Be active with your management and discuss various marketing strategies. Because in many cases, non-marketing specialists does not know many concepts and strategies of marketing, sales and procurement.

This will help you to build good relationships with management and team, who will support you in any proposal to take over a market.

5) Provide ideas to your management on various areas of activity of the company.

For example, during discussion with my chairman I asked the pricing of the flour. He said that they bought it from a dealer for 250 local units. As a specialist, I was knowing all the prices in the market. I said that I knew where our company could buy for 190 local units. My chairman was surprised and did not believe me first time. He ordered other managers to go with me and check the pricing. After we checked. My chairman made an order to higher my position to the senior manager with responsibilities in purchasing.

6) Learn the language of your company. One of the languages of my first company was Foreign Language which I had never learned before. I was so curious as a marketing specialist that I bought several books and start learning it during nights and weekends. After 3 months, I could speak with many specialists without translator. It helped me to talk directly on key issues of pricing and general communication.

7) Explore new markets.
   As I analyzed several markets abroad and talked to wholesalers, I knew the pricing of the neighbor markets and also in cities at the distance from

more than 300-500 km. from our factory. So, I proposed to take and develop our distribution channels there. My company chairman supported me and after short time we invited 2 distributors for a new region.

8) Explore and develop yourself.

I had a bachelor degree when I was the marketing specialist in my joint venture. But I wanted to continue my education. One day, I explained my chairman about my future goals and he supported me and asked to apply for master degree program. It was so motivating for me. So, I joined my master program in one of the local universities where I started to learn marketing management. Working and doing my master degree at the same time.

In these ways, I practiced marketing in my best way to explore, learn and develop in many companies I joined. It helped me to grow as a marketing professional at the end.

And after so many years, it allows me to share my experiences with you in this book.

Marketing Professional

When you have more than 5 years of true experience in one field, you become a professional. No matter of your field of work.

When you are professional, it does not denote that you have to stop your learning, developing and sharing in marketing or any other subject. Actually, you have to do twice more than you were doing before. Because, markets and environments, as technologies and equipment, are changing very fast.

Here, I would like to provide my best tips and strategies for the professionals in order to stay fit:

1) Become a member of various professional associations in many fields. It will help you to stay in the new trends.
2) Read books: fictional and non-fictional. It helps you expand your horizon of thinking and development.

3) Do some testing. There are many web-sites, where you can check your marketing skills by testing yourself.

4) Join professional clubs for various activities with professionals and specialists like you.

5) Organize your events, including forums, conferences, round tables and presentations.

6) Join universities or colleges for teaching and research. Universities and colleges are the best places to get innovative ideas for your businesses and career.

7) Invest and launch companies, projects. The best professional should be independent of any salary sources and income.

8) Do research and write articles and publish them in newspapers, magazines and online.

9) Write books and publish them on www.amazon.com. You will not only

become an expert, but also earn royalty.

10) Look for opportunities abroad. There are many chances to get new contracts for your company services or consulting.

11) Become a speaker at various events and forums to share your ideas and experiences.

12) Open your personal blog or web-site to promote your ideas, concepts, books and services for the public. Now you can help many companies and organizations as a professional.

Every year your expertise and knowledge will grow, and in one day, you will become a marketing *guru*.

I wish you all the best and become a marketing *guru*. I hope my book will be one of the motivations for it.

Marketing Terms

As a marketing student, it is important to learn many marketing terms. Some of them have a conceptual meaning and application, and some of them can be used as necessary theoretical and practical tools.

As a marketing student you can review many terms very easily. If you know the mentioned terms of this book – you are an excellent specialist! You are the best marketing specialist I have ever met! It means that you have studied well at your university or workplace!

If you do not! Do not worry! This book will help you to remind and help you to learn.

All of the terms are generated from my classical marketing books and also from practical experience as a marketing manager, including in online projects. Generally, these terms are explained to you from my own words.

1. SWOT Analysis

This is a classical analysis of the internal and external factors of the organization. The uppercase letters mean:

S - Strengths

W - Weaknesses

O – Opportunities

T - Threats

2. STEP Analysis

STEP analysis refers to the analysis of macro environment of the organizations. The uppercase letters mean:

S – Social factors

T – Technological factor

E – Economic factor

P – Political factor

3. AIDA

AIDA – is a model of communication influence, which refers to:

A – Attention

I – Interest

D – Desire

A – Action

There is also an additional element such as:

A – Additional Action

4. Marketing Mix

Marketing mix is a term developed by the American Marketing Association in 1950. It describes how marketing specialists make decisions on key elements of the marketing plan. The classical terms are still used and have extended versions.

5. 4P Marketing Mix

4P Marketing Mix is a marketing model used in marketing of products, which refers to:

-Product

-Place

-Price

-Promotion

6. The extended 8P Marketing Mix

This is an extended marketing mix tool used in marketing of products. It refers to:

-Product

-Place

-Price

-Promotion

-People

-Processes

-Physical Evidence

-Productivity and Quality

7. 4C Marketing Mix

4C Marketing Mix is a marketing model used in marketing of products, which means:

-Customer

-Convenience

-Cost

-Communication

8. BCG Matrix

BCG Matrix is a chart, which helps to define strategies based on relations of the market growth and relative market share. It was developed by the Boston Consulting Group in 1968.

Table 6 BCG Matrix

		Market Share	
		High	Low
Market Growth	High	Star	Problem Child
	Low	Cash Cow	Dog

Each window stands for the following meaning:

Stars – high share and high growth markets

Cash Cow – high share but low growth market

Dog – low share and low growth market

Problem child – low share and high growth market

9. Advertising

Advertising is a marketing communication tool which defines and promotes a product or service through paid media channels.

10. Bottleneck

Bottleneck is usually called a situation when the performance of the system is limited by one element in the process. The best example of creating a bottleneck effect is a theater and its exit doors in the hall after the ending of the performance.

11. Customer Decision Making

Customer Decision Making – is a process of the customer experience to decide on becoming a customer. It consists of 3 main stages:

-Awareness

-Evaluation

-Conversion

12. Awareness

Awareness – is a stage when a potential customer should be aware about the need or problem and about your company, which has the product or service to satisfy a need or solve a problem.

13. Evaluation

Evaluation – is a stage when a potential customer should have a chance to evaluate various options, including the competitive products in the market and all other opportunities.

14. Conversion

Conversion – is a stage when a potential customer decides to become a customer and buy your product or service.

15. Funnel

Funnel is a sales channel of how your content should be developed to facilitate your awareness, evaluation and conversion.

It is actually an entire marketing process of the content in the company.

There are three types of content funnels.

- TOFU (top of the funnel), which facilitates awareness.
- MOFU (middle of the funnel), which facilitates evaluation.
- BOFU (bottom of the funnel), which facilitates conversion.

16. Top of the Funnel

At this stage, potential customers are interested in your news, blogs, podcasts, social media pages, infographics, photographs, books, digital magazines, newsletters, web-site, research reports etc.

17. Middle of the funnel

At this stage, customers are interested in educational and help resources, discount, coupons, surveys, webinars, quizzes, databases etc. They usually want to see more content about your company and products.

18. Bottom of the funnel

At this stage, potential customers are interested in a free trial, demo version, customer story, comparison, spec sheet, webinar, event, free class or free consultation etc.

19. ATL

ATL stands for Above the Line Advertising, where mass media is used to promote the products or services. Examples of ATL Advertisement are TV, radio, print and internet.

20. BTL

BTL stands for below the line advertising, where advertising is one to one to the customer. Examples of BTL are emailing, direct sales, booklets, personal consulting, and etc.

21. Benchmarking

Benchmarking – is a process of comparing and evaluating best companies' products, services and processes and other metrics with your own in order to define improvement opportunities for the market leadership.

22. Brand

Unique characteristic, logo or trademark that brings about awareness of a specific product, service or business while differentiating it from other products or services.

23. B2G

It means Business to Government and refers the relationship between business and government in purchasing of goods and services. This is often referred as marketing of a public sector.

24. B2B

B2B means Business to Business. It refers a business relationship between business and another business, which markets to it raw materials, resources, semi-products or services.

25. B2C

B2C means Business to Customer and it refers describing a business that sells to consumers a final good or service for consumption.

26. Business Model

Business model is a structure, which means how company operate, build processes, do finances and make revenues and generate profits.

There are many types of business models are now available in the market, including digital business models, which become more popular.

Main business models include the following: Inventor, Manufacturer, Distributor, Trader, Wholesaler, Retailer, Advertisement, Affiliate Marketing, Franchiser, Drop shipping, Crowdsourcing Brick and Mortar, Portal, eCommerce, Online Marketplace, Blockchain, Brick and Clicks, Nickel and Dime, Freemium, Subscription, Aggregator,

Data Licensing, Data Selling, Agency Based, SAAS, IASS, PAAS, High Touch, Low Touch, Startup, Entrepreneur, Broker, Landlord, Creditor, Contractor and others.

27. CMS

CMS is a Content Management System, which is an administrator tool that helps to manage all the functions and sections for creating the content on the web-site. These may include setting up, editing, publishing, indexing, navigational elements, etc.

28. CRM

CRM means customer relationship management, which is a system that helps you organize all of your marketing and sales activities, including storing contact information, tracking emails, storing deals, and more.

29. Digital Marketing

Digital marketing is any online marketing activity, focusing on reaching a target audience. This includes internet research, online advertising, email marketing, content marketing, search engine optimization, social media marketing etc.

30. Direct Marketing

Direct Marketing means dealing directly with the customer rather than via a medium party. Also, it means directly communicating with your target audience. Types of direct marketing are advertising, presentation or office sales.

31. E-Commerce

E-commerce is a business model which refers to the selling of products digitally on the internet.

32. Export Marketing

Export Marketing is an activity of focusing on entry strategies and development in new export markets.

33. Inbound Marketing

Inbound Marketing means promoting and advertising your company or products via content marketing, podcasts, video, eBooks, email broadcast, SEO, Social Marketing, etc. An ideal customer should find you via interacting with your content, searching by keywords, tags and etc.

34. Infographic

Infographic is a type of visual content, which aims at making complex information easy to understand and perceive.

35. International Marketing

International marketing is a marketing activity done on international level, taking into account country specific issues, channels, traditions etc.

36. KPI

KPI stands for Key Performance Indicator and is a measure of the performance of various activities, factors, employees, marketing actions etc. KPIs helps organizations to achieve their goals by constantly analyzing the indicators.

37. Lifetime Customer Value

Lifetime Customer Value is a value of the customer in net profit, attributed to the entire future relationship and purchases of the customer.

38. Marketing Communication

It is a process of selecting and communicating with your customers via messages and channels. Marketing communication can include advertising, branding, marketing mix, direct marketing, exporting, packaging, PR, digital media, content management etc.

39. Market Segmentation

It is diving your market into the groups based on geographic, socio-economic, cultural, demographic etc. factors. It will help at the end to define your target markets in each group.

40. Marketing Automation

This is the tool that lets you automate your marketing reports, activities, campaigns. For example, through lead development, behavior-based strategies, you can automate sending marketing messages to the target audience at the right time.

41. Marketing Research

Marketing Research is an analytical process over a specific industry for the development of new solutions, products or business decisions.

42. Marketing

Marketing is the process of identifying, anticipating and satisfying customer requirements in a profitable way.

43. Market Niche

A very specific segment of a market in which you can meet the needs of your customers in the best way.

44. New Product Development

The creation of a new product that involves research, development, product testing and launching.

45. Outbound Marketing

Outbound marketing refers to a traditional form of marketing when a company sends its message to an audience. It can be TV or radio commercial, print ads, tradeshows, conference and etc.

46. Pricing

Pricing is a marketing process of defining a value of your goods in terms of money. It can be based on costs, perceived value, comparative pricing, market prices and freemium.

47. PR

PR refers to public relations and is a marketing communication tool to build relations with the public and strengthen company image and publicity. It consists of media releases, conferences, social images, etc., that make up and maintain the reputation of an organization and its brands.

48. Product Lifecycle

Product Lifecycle is a description of the entire process of stages, in which the product goes from research and development to growth, maturity and decline. Each stage has its own association and market changes, which should be a signal for marketing specialists to change their marketing strategies and marketing mix models.

49. R&D

R&D means Research and Development, which is a process of discovering and developing new inventions, products and services.

50. ROI

ROI means return on investment, which is measure of the profitability of the investment in marketing, sales, etc. If the ROI on an investment is negative, it generally means you're losing money on that business. Measuring the ROI on marketing efforts helps to ensure that you're investing your money into the strategies that bring results.

51. Sales

Sales is an activity of marketing products and services at the point of sales in a given period of time. There are many sales techniques and strategies. The most popular are: SPIN selling, SNAP selling, Challenger Sale, Sandler Sale, Consultative or Solution Sale.

52. SEO

SEO is a Search Engine Optimization, which is a method to increase a webpage's performance in web search results via focusing on keywords, title and image tags, links, and more.

53. Social Media

Social Media are platforms like Facebook, Twitter, LinkedIn, Instagram and

Snapchat that help connect with potential customers and public. Marketers use these networks to increase awareness, grow their customer base and achieve business goals.

54. Website

A web-site is a company identification page on the internet to build awareness and promote the company, its products and services. It can include pages like: contact us, about us, products and services etc.

Marketing Strategies

There are many marketing strategies to start supporting your business or organization. Marketing strategies are useful not only for promoting company, products or services, but also for brand building, promotion of government reputation and also one's personal image.

Here, in this section, I will try to advice you with the most common and popular marketing strategies taking into account new trends and my own experience.

Let's start with them.

1. Create a web-site

It is important to launch a web-site of the company with your own corporate name and logo as the first step. Any customer should find your company via search engines to learn your services and products, as well as portfolio and staff. In digital era, it is especially vital to be online to communicate with your customers and react to the complains instantly. If not, they cost your business and your future a lot of money and even your future.

2. Use social media marketing

Using social networks will help your business grow faster by increasing your followers – potential customers, partners and suppliers. It will help you to launch targeted messages for your specific audiences in various market segments.

3. Begin your blog

Many customers make decisions on how company leaders and employees think, including their relations to the customers, business environment, ecology etc.

Blogs can show your face and internal life and where you are heading with your products to solve a problem or bring a new solution.

4. Utilize SEO

Every day millions of people search for their products and services online. SEO will help you to find your clients easily. Keywords, tags, titles will help your clients find their solutions in your web-site effectively.

5. Create an affiliate program

Today, by experiencing with your products your customers can earn money. For that they can share their views about your products purchased, links and advantages. It is important to learn a whole value chain of the affiliate program. You and your customers have to benefit from it, especially loyal customers.

6. Export your products

There are many countries where your product or service can find its new customers and become more demanding. With available marketing tools and techniques, you can focus on how to export your product or service abroad and earn greater value.

For exporting, you have to understand the specific features of markets, INCORTERMS, cost of transportation and logistics, certifications, the tariffs and other costs of entry.

7. Invest in R&D

Every product and service in a competitive market has a limited life cycle. Learn how to expand in R&D to extend your product life cycle or create a new one. Without any secret, your long-term value creation depends on R&D in many cases.

8. Create knowledge systems

In a complex world of technologies, it is difficult for customers to understand the full value of your product at once. Creating tips, tutorials, Q&A and interactive contents will help them to understand your products and services well.

Building a knowledge system should start with creating databases, research materials, educational and training programs, articles, publications, news, infographics, contracts and etc.

9. Build systems for investors

Any business project requires investments for R&D, for growing and developing, especially innovative products. Learn how to attract investors, including international financial institutions, foreign direct investment and funding.

There are many ways to attract investments. You have to learn them and apply in your business models.

Regarding projects, the best way is to learn how to make projects based on international standards and offer them investors focusing on profitable one.

10. Focus on content creation

Almost all people make decision on purchase based on available information about the products, reviews and experiences.

But if your product is a new one and you do not have any review from your customer, it is better to show your product or service from the point of usability, laboratory tests etc.

It is all about content creation from what you have, for example, from laboratory tests or video materials.

Marketing Plan

The outcome of your marketing activity can be improved by marketing plan indicators.

Any plan is a necessary element of realizing your goals, strategies and tactics with important indicators to achieve.

Therefore, start you marketing actions or campaigns with marketing planning.

Generally, any marketing plan consists of the following sections:

- Executive Summary
- Mission Statement
- Goals and Tasks
- Standards of Performance
- Core Competencies
- SWOT analysis
- Buyer Persona
- Target Market
- Marketing Mix
    - Product
    - Place
    - Pricing

- Promotion
- People
- Processes
- Physical Evidence
- Productivity

- Marketing Strategies

- Risks

- Budget

- KPI

Above sections are sample sections of the marketing plan, however. Depending on the company products and services, this plan structure can be adapted.

You can design your marketing plan using traditional and modern elements. For example, in the digital era, you can actively focus on digital channels and instruments to get higher scope of your work online.

For marketing students, it is important to learn how to structure a marketing plan, find necessary information and use this information to write the sections of the plan for decision makers.

How to increase your researcher ranking?

While studying you can do your research and write your articles and publications. Placing your publications in the well-known and international journals with the high Impact Factor or H-index can increase your ranking.

As a marketing student, you can ask your professor to supervise you to write joint articles and research papers.

Generally, in order to increase your ranking as researcher, you can apply the following strategies:

1) Write your articles and place them in the open source journals, Academia.edu, EBSCO etc.
2) Review the articles of other authors and comment them. It will also increase your ranking.
3) Join as an assistant of your professor and start doing some research for your professor's book or article.

4) Register for a membership in the marketing associations to participate in the events, where you can meet marketing specialists to do the joint research projects or marketing research.
5) Initiate your University Researcher Club, for example, to involve other students for joint research projects. After launching your club, you can work on searching for funding together with your professors and students.
6) Participate in the international events, conferences and forums and make speeches about your marketing topics or research.
7) Constantly analyze market data and make tables of analysis to compare and write reports about key issues of the economy and business marketing.
8) Start writing books about marketing areas and other topics. You will need

a lot of research work and analysis for that.

There are many ways to do your research and become the best researcher. You have to understand yourself first, allocate your time for research and select the best way to fit your character and professional research skills.

Generally, your research experience will help you in marketing planning and in outcomes of all your marketing actions and campaigns.

How to write effectively?

Many young students today in many countries have writing problems. Especially in English Language.

The following points are the writing tips and steps to improve writing preparation and skills.

1) Think about the topic from a far.
   To do that, find your best place and relax. Make your ideas flow from a long-lasting idea or a serious issue you have noticed recently or in the past.
2) Define the structure, audience and key sections of the paper.
3) Write down your main ideas and notes.
4) Make a plan for your writing, including how much time you will devote your time.
5) Review books, articles and browse an internet for information and ideas, statistics and main concepts.
6) Write your first draft.

7) If you use ideas and concepts from literature cite them in an appropriate way, according to international standards.
8) Do not afraid to make mistakes or misuses. The best writing is when you review your work several times, before it will go for evaluation and publication.
9) Do not plagiarize and copy past from internet.
10) Review your sections for flow, connection of sections, and how it achieves the purpose of the book.
11) Add new or updated points, concepts, conclusions or recommendations.
12) Proofread several times for mistakes, misunderstandings or usage of words, sentences, grammar etc.
13) Write down your conclusion and recommendations.

14) In the final stage, write a summary, description, abstract or outline. It should be attractive for your readers' attention and as the first reading section.
15) For internet publication, write down and select 10 keywords based on analysis in search engines.

For creative writing it is important to feel your audience and make them emotional while reading your work.

How to present successfully your work?

In marketing classes, we have a lot of presentation work by students. They present their business ideas, homework, case studies, projects etc. Unfortunately, even today many students face difficulty.

I remember that in my personal life, nobody taught me either how to present on the stage or in the class. I learned everything in practice and by tips of my classmates or professors.

So, I hope with this book, I can help my students and many other people with the tips to progress in presentation of their materials. As a marketing specialist they have to learn how to present the company products or services in the region or in the international arena.

The following are the tips and steps for your best outcome in presentation:

1) Think about the presentation and its main ideas.
2) Define the topic of your presentation.
3) Make notes about your topic.
4) Review literature.
5) Make a plan of your presentation.
6) Compile your slides and content.
7) Prepare your first draft of the presentation.
8) Make calculations if it requires. Put them in the slides in the appropriate form.
9) Review your slides and text for mistakes, grammar, use of words, sentences etc.
10) Prepare your possible questions and answers to be ready to answer for any comments or questions from your audience.
11) Prepare your speech also.
12) Save the final and print out the presentation for your audience and for yourself. Include also your notes or speech text for you.

13) Make sure that your presentation has interactivity and storytelling component.

14) In the presentation day, be early in the class, where you will be presenting. Prepare everything in the best format and quality. Make sure that microphone and dynamics are working.

15) Start your presentation with pause to draw the attention of the audience.

16) Eye check your audience and try to understand participants' emotions, feelings etc.

17) Ask your audience about how they feel and what they are expecting from your presentation. If possible, draw on the blackboard to count their expectations. But do not forget to evaluate them after the presentation.

18) Try to interact with your audience as much as possible to lead the flow.

19) Make main points of your presentation and pause for explanation, questions or additional links or ideas.
20) Finish your presentation with your ideas and recommendations.
21) Go to the blackboard and tick the points where you achieved expectations of your audience. Check whether all points are ticked or not. Try to answer to those that are not covered.
22) Finally, thank your audience and answer questions.
23) As a last step, submit your materials to your professor for evaluation.

How to read efficiently?

Students have to read a lot of books to prepare for their classes and exams. Many of them spend too much time on their key classes and other classes they ignore with no time for reading.

I had the same situation when I was studying at university. And to improve reading skills by many times the focus was on meanings and strategies rather than on word counting.

So, below are the best strategies to learn reading efficiently and know the subject very well.

1. First read the questions at the end of the chapter.
2. Read the conclusion of each chapter if any.
3. Read the first paragraph and the last one to get the meaning. Think and conclude the meaning of the whole chapter.
4. Next, go quickly through the whole chapter and try to understand the

main sections, tables, graphs, keywords if any.

5. Next time, go through each paragraph for 5-10 seconds and try to remember the main words and meaning, connecting them with the meaning of the first and last paragraphs. If it is not clear, read the first and the last sentence of each paragraph.

These are the strategies for quick reading of any additional material or book.

Course Book Reading

For course book, read it by taking a pencil at hand. Underline important sentences and make notes in the book. For example, to save book for many other students in future, I made notes at my notebook.

For example, I write down main definitions, explanations, conclusions or terms from the book.

All this important if you want to read and remember your writings for future, especially, for your exam preparation.

Fast Reading Timer

To constantly improve your reading by speed. Check timer and try to read and count not your words per minute but the volume of reading.

Make a plan for fast reading. Practice for understanding the meaning of paragraph in one minute.

How to be active in class participation?

Class participation depends on preparation of the student for the class or by the background and the speaking skills.

Every professor wants students to be active in discussions. In this way, they learn how to speak in the public, defend their ideas and clearly present them.

To be active in the class, it is better if a student has already read the class material. So, it is important that students receive their materials at the beginning of their semester. For example, course books.

The following are the best strategies for the class participation.

1. Do your homework reading and tasks.
2. Read your course book of your class by fast reading strategy.
3. Make notes of the chapter.
4. Prepare questions to ask professor.

5. Analyze information on the internet and print out. For example, if the topic is Marketing Mix, you can find a company, which implemented 7P in your city or around the world. You can present your findings to the class.
6. Make your main conclusions about the chapter to share with your classmates and professor.

How to prepare for exams?

Preparation to the exams can be time consuming and stressful.

The best strategies for the exams are the following:

1. Ask about the exam format and sample questions from your professor for each subject.
2. Take your exam questions 2-3 weeks before the exam date.
3. Allocate your time for every day. For example, 2-3 hours to prepare for your exams.
4. Make a plan of preparation for each subject (see below).

Table 7 Sample Exam Preparation Plan

Subjects	Exam Date	Allocation of time per day for preparation	Period
Marketing	Dec. 15	15 min	14:50-15:30
Economics	Dec. 19	20 min	17:40-18:20

| Finance | Dec. 20 | 30 min | 20:00-20:45 |
| Language | Dec. 21 | 10 min | 22:00-22:30 |

5. Try to understand the questions first and the professor's logic of compiling the questions.
6. Review your class notes.
7. Review your book.
8. Review your lecture notes as well.
9. Practice on learning main definitions, graphs, charts, tables etc. by fast reading.
10. For calculation subjects like statistics, finance, when you have to do profit or cost calculation, try to practice by solving tasks as many as possible.
11. After going through all the book, review all the sections again with a faster speed. Stop on the definitions but close the paragraph and try to answer yourself the main meaning by writing or by closing your eyes. Check the book and evaluate how you

remembered the meaning. If not, try to read and remember once more.

12. Review until you will know the main concepts, terms, graphs etc. of the course book 100%.

13. Practice on writing answers to the questions by your own words based on course book, experiences and new ideas from the class.

14. Check out a sample test book about marketing and do as many tests as possible.

How to get funding when you are student?

Many students ask me, how to get funding for the project they have in their mind.

Actually, I like this question as I work in financial sector too. We allocate state budgets and support social and entrepreneurial projects. From last year we support also youth projects and provide them soft loans for starting their business projects.

However, many other financial sources are available for students to support their study period, exchange program, research papers, realization of their projects and in many other areas.

Let me list the strategies and tips to succeed in attracting funding.

1) Check out scholarships. If you need financial aid for your study period go through the university web-site. There are also many organizations

provide financial support based on academic, sports or research merit. There are also need based scholarships are available. Please ask your university supervisor and try to look for yourself in the internet.

However, students have to understand requirements to apply for any scholarship.

2) Participate in contests. Prizes for participation in various student contests or competitions, including in sports and writing are available. For example, writing contest can provide prizes from USD100 to up to USD10,000.

3) Check grants. Grants for research projects are available from many companies, non-governmental and governmental sources. If students or teams with professors defend their project well, organization may allocate grants for 2-3 years. For

example, research grants can be up to USD100 000 or even more.

4) Check for grants from ministry of education of your country, international organizations or universities for exchange programs, master degrees or PhD programs etc.

5) Find your student job. Depending on your time management, you can still do your work as a student in the university or company nearby your university/dormitory. You can also do your job as a freelancer online. For example, if you are a professional at designing, writing or marketing, you can easily find orders in freelancer portals.

6) There are also loans for study. But I am not recommending loans for studentship or any research projects. It takes your nerves and can be risky to repay while you are studying. You can take loans for business projects only.

Sample Marketing Tests

So, we are almost in the final stage of our handbook for marketing students. Let's evaluate your readings.

As a practical tool, you can find below some test questions for your review. Please answer them and check the right answers after. Wish you all the best!

1) .... is comparing ones business processes and performance metrics to industry and other company best practices.
   Please enter missing word from the list below:
   A) SWOT
   B) Benchmarking
   C) PEST Analysis
   D) Technical Analysis

2) Strategies that focus on reduction of time needed to accomplish the task is defined as
   ....
   A) Time-based strategies
   B) Quality-based strategies
   C) Agile Operations
   D) Service-based strategies

3) Change management is ....
   A) a study about how money is managed the process of acquiring needed time

B) a systematic approach to dealing with the transition of an organization's goals, processes and technologies
C) a measure of effective use of resources
D) an approach, used to guide the operations function

4) Which factor is not included in 7S of the McKinsey model that effect the change?
   A) Shared Value
   B) Strategy
   C) Structure
   D) Supply

5) Which is not included in 4P Model of the Marketing?
   A) Product
   B) People
   C) Place
   D) Price

6) Which is not included in the 4C Model of the Marketing?
   A) Cost
   B) Convenience
   C) Communication
   D) Coordination

7) A measure is expressed as the ratio of output to inputs used in a production process, i.e. output per unit of input:
   A) Efficiency
   B) Productivity
   C) Quality
   D) Profitability

8) From below, what is not a factor for change?
   A) Changing Customer Demand
   B) Changing Technology
   C) Changing Competition
   D) New Product of your company

9) In SWOT it analyzes the company possibilities to grow in the target markets. What is this?

   A) Strengths
   B) Weaknesses
   C) Opportunities
   D) Threats

10) What is the main trend the global economy faces nowadays?

   A) Digitalization
   B) Gasification
   C) Financial boom
   D) Electrification

11) CRM – is a ???:
   A) Cost Relationship Management
   B) Customer Relationship Management
   C) Customer Relationship Marketing
   D) Competitor Relationship Management

12) Define 3 main competitive advantages of your product or service. And briefly explain. Why product/service needs change? (Use additional paper, it is not counted as a test question).

Answers:

1. B
2. A
3. B
4. D
5. B
6. D
7. B
8. D
9. C
10. A
11. B

Evaluate yourself

1) Constantly evaluate yourself to understand your efficiency as a student and specialist.

2) Analyze constantly vacancies and check whether you have such skills. If not, focus during your university to learn new skills.

3) Improve your language and professional skills by participating in various Language Clubs, Trainings and Seminars.

4) Analyze your health and do your sport activities to stay fit and healthy.

5) Evaluate yourself on time management. Make priorities and focus if you are out of time or too stressful with many works at once.

6) Learn how to say "no" to your classmates, friends or fellows to plan your student day.

7) Be organized, punctual and responsible with meetings, classes and homework.

8) Be responsible for your words and wishes.
9) Constantly make a list of wishes and try to achieve them.
10) If you have free time, learn how to spend your time effectively and earn some money.
11) Be prepared to be confident in communication and in presentation.
12) Take initiative to join projects, contests or various student activities.
13) Be open for professors and students as only they can support you during your study period.

Tips for parents

University students are independent enough but, in many cultures, especially in eastern and Asian, student still rely on parents.

It is important that parents control them and show the road for their success too.

There are some tips for parents, how to help to your children to be independent, successful and responsible. Check them out below:

1) Ask your student about his success at university once a week.
2) To make your adult responsible, ask him verbally to make a report about what he/she was done for the last month.
3) Do not give your car key or any other expensive gadget, until he will not get the best grade in all classes.
4) Ask your student whether he is involved in other activities at the university. Based on this book's tips

for students, recommend your student to join various activities!

5) Check the grades of your student monthly!

6) Do a homework with him once in quarter.

7) If your mature has difficulty spending too much time in front of a computer or under the books, let him/her know how to take breaks every 50 minutes and do some physical exercises in between.

8) If your student comes very late every day, ask him where he/she was and why he/she is late. Make sure that he/she does not spend too much time in computer game clubs, night clubs or somewhere else. Many students during free university life can join various groups and organizations, including those where they accustom for drinking alcohol, taking narcotics or other bad habits.

9) Many parents allow their children to work and earn some money because of financial situation. Make sure that your children are not all the time at work in order to earn money. They have to attend classes and participate to get better grades.

10) Check constantly about the books your student is reading. Praise him for buying books or reading. During university life your student should be busy with reading, research and public activities.

11) Learn your student's habit and thinking, as in university he/she will form new character. Learn how to motivate and support your mature for new achievements.

Tip for professors and lecturers

My management skills to control my staff in my companies helped me to control the students as well.

I would like to share some of the most useful tips to improve students' motivation and involvement for my colleagues.

1) Never be late to your class and teach students not to be late as well. In some cultures, especially in Eastern, Muslim and Asian, punctuality is a serious problem.
2) Be prepared for each class.
3) Make additional materials such as your presentations, business cases and other materials available for your students.
4) Inform students in time about your activities and plans for the next class.
5) Send your students all main materials of the class, including course books in the beginning of the semester.

6) Interact your students with Q&A, business cases, presentations, discussions etc.

7) It is important for students to focus on writing tasks during the class and explain how they can improve their writing skills. Most of the students are struggling with writing and they need your support.

   Generally, this book provides many tips for improving professional skills of the student.

8) Allow students flexibility. For example, they can ask you to do another homework task or prepare some research paper by their own initiative.

9) Try to organize classes with inviting speakers from companies or organize company visits to listen true success stories or show students the real production or retail chain.

10) Test your students every 3-4 weeks on how they remembered the materials of the class.

11) Evaluate your students based on fair grading scale. Give them bonuses as much as possible.

12) Check any contribution in the table designed (active participation, projects, presentations, tests, other class and homework tasks). You can check the sample table below from my marketing class (see Figure below).

Figure 1 Student Evaluation Sheet

Student Grade Table

№	Full name	25.1 A1	A2	1.2 A1	A2	8.2 A1	A2	15.2 A1	A2	22.2 A1	A2	1.3 A1	A2	15.3 A1	A2	29.3 A1	A2	5.4 A1	A2	13.4 A1	A2	Project C	P	HW 1	2	3	Test/Classwork 1	2	3	TS	%	Min	Max
1	Anuarova Bainur	3	3	3	3	3	3	4	3	4	6	4	3	4	3										7		8			64	64%	55	100
2	Altavarova Karina	5	4	5	4	4	4	4	5	5	10	5	5	5	5							10					11	10	5	106	100%	55	100
3	Bakbergenov Abylaykhan	4	4	4	4	6	5	5	5	10	4	5	6	6										5			11	10	5	101	101%	55	100
4	Berdibek Adilet	4	4	4	5			5	3	5	10			4	4									5	10		11	10	10	94	94%	55	100
5	Duysenbekova Symbat	3	4					3	3	4	6	3	4	4	4							6		10			8			62	62%	55	100
6	Esenaliuly Raskhat	5	4	5	4	5	4	5	5	10	4	5	3	3													11	10	5	92	92%	55	100
7	Ali Asani Talgatovna	3	4	3	3	3	5	3	4	6	5	3	5	3													8			80	80%	55	100
8	Kim Konstantin	3	3	3	3	3	3	4	6	3	3	3	3											5			4			59	59%	55	100
9	Oralbay Nurbolat	3	3			4	5	4	6	5	5													10	10			10	10	74	74%	55	100
10	Ory-bek Nursultan	4	4	4	4	4	5	5	5	10	4	5										5					11	5	10	89	89%	55	100
11	Tojiev Murat	4	4	4	3	4	4			4	6	4	5	4	4									5	5		10	10		80	80%	55	100
12	Tursynbek Alenur			5	4	4	5	5	5	5	10											10		10			5	5	5	78	78%	55	100
13	Ustimenko Irina	5	4	5	4	5	4			5	10			5	5							10		10					10	5	87	87%	55	100
14	Orhan Ulchan	4	3			4	3			4	6	5	5									7		7			7	7		62	62%	55	100

Blue-the best (above 100%) A1-attendance (minus if late)
Green-excellent (85-100%) A2-participation
Yellow-good (70-84%)
Orange-satisfactory (55-69%)
Red-poor

C-content
P-presentation
B-bonus
TS-total score
HW-homework
Min-55%
Max-100%
company visit
class work

About author

Nigel Aksel is a marketing specialist with more than 20 years of experience in marketing, online activities and management. He is involved as a lecturer of marketing and project management at the South-Kazakhstan State University.

Nigel is a founder of several organizations and projects in several countries. He enjoys writing about multiple issues of university life, education and science. As a member of educational institutions, he understands well about the problems of education and science in CIS countries. He knows many areas of management and strategies how to improve the situation to help the local universities to adapt to the international level.

Where can you find interesting stories about investments, export and trade on the internet?

Nurbek Achilov has some resources for you!

On Blogger's platform he runs his blog about investments, export, trade and other issues.

Blog about investment, export and trade in English:

https://nurbekachilov.blogspot.com/

Blog about investment, export and trade in English:

https://nurbekachil.blogspot.com/

You can also find ideas, photos and experiences about investments, trade and investment on Nurbek Achilov's pages in Facebook, Instagram, Pinterest, Slideshare, Academia and LinkedIn and other accounts.

orcid.org/0000-0003-1238-6556

Kazakhstan

Tips for Travelers

Nurbek Achilov

Second Edition

Get my new book with the Special Price on
Amazon.com

---

*200 web-sites and tools for online
presence*

Essential Handbook for marketing and growth

Nurbek Achilov

First Edition